EDGE BOOKS™

BIZARRE THINGS WE'VE DONE FOR SPORT

BY TYLER OMOTH

Consultant:
Eric Allen Hall, Ph.D.
Assistant Professor, History
Georgia Southern University
Statesboro, Georgia

CAPSTONE PRESS
a capstone imprint

Edge Books are published by Capstone Press,
1710 Roe Crest Drive, North Mankato, Minnesota 56003
www.capstonepub.com

Library of Congress Cataloging-in-Publication Data
Cataloging-in-Publication data is on file with the Library of Congress.
ISBN 978-1-4914-4267-8 (library binding)
ISBN 978-1-4914-4343-9 (paperback)
ISBN 978-1-4914-4323-1 (eBook PDF)

Developed and Produced by Focus Strategic Communications, Inc.
Adrianna Edwards: project manager
Ron Edwards: editor
Rob Scanlan: designer and compositor
Mary Rose MacLachlan: media researcher
Francine Geraci: copy editor and proofreader
Wendy Scavuzzo: fact checker

Photo Credits
Alamy: imageimage, 13, Lesley Pardoe, 17, Nick Gammon, 21, Stephen Dorey ABIPP, 18–19; Dreamstime: Steeve
Dubois, 18 (inset); Glow Images: ImageBroker, 14, Stock Connection/View Stock, 7 (top); iStockphoto: SDAM,
6; Newscom: EPA/Alex Hofford, 8, EPA/Markku Ojala, 9, EPA/Miguel Sierra, 15, Eye Ubiquitous, 22, MCT/
Chuck Myers, 7 (bottom), UPI/Art Foxall, 12; North Wind Picture Archives, 25; Shutterstock: Arne Bramsen, 26,
Dawid Lech, 4–5, Fotokvadrat, 24, homydesign, 20, Jelena Aloskina, 27, Photoprofi30, 28, Sean Donohue Photo, 10,
topten22photo, cover, 11, wabang70, 16; Wikimedia: Poniol60, 29

Design Elements by Shutterstock

Printed in the United States of America in North Mankato, Minnesota.
042015   00823CGF15

TABLE OF CONTENTS

PAIN AND DANGER FOR SPORT

You sit on your horse with your lance and shield in hand. The roar of the crowd sounds like thunder. You look across the field and see your **opponent**. He also holds a lance and shield. The flag drops and you kick your heels into your horse. As you get closer, you aim your lance directly at your opponent. Bang! His lance drives into your shoulder. But you manage to stay on your horse. Your lance strikes him and sends him flying, crashing painfully to the ground. You have won the **jousting tournament**. But that really hurt!

Sports are a huge part of human culture. Ancient cave paintings show wrestling matches and other contests. Competing with others is a part of human nature. But sometimes we go to extremes. There have been and still are some odd sports. Some can even be dangerous or deadly.

opponent—a person who competes against another person
jousting—fighting between two knights on horseback with long spears called lances
tournament—a series of matches between several players or teams, ending in one winner

Medieval jousting competitions are recreated today at Renaissance fairs.

CHAPTER 1

THAT IS JUST SILLY!

People have always gathered to enjoy sports. Games that require physical strength, speed, and **stamina** draw **spectators** as well as contestants. The desire for new sports has led people to create new ways to compete, such as snowboarding or disc golf. Other people may look at these sports and think, "That is just silly!"

> **stamina**—the energy and strength to keep doing something for a long time
> **spectator**—a person who attends and watches an event

In disc golf, also known as frisbee golf or frolf, players throw a plastic disc at a target.

The Naked Olympics

This Ancient Greek pot shows men sprinting.

The first Olympic Games were held in Ancient Greece around the year 776 BC. There was only one event—a simple 600-foot (183-meter) race. Only men competed. The winner was a cook named Koroibos. What is so silly about that? These early Olympic athletes ran completely naked!

THE OLYMPIC GAMES

The Olympic Games have a long and interesting history. Since 1896, the games have been held every four years. The 1896 Games were held in Athens, Greece. There were 43 different events. Today the Summer and Winter Games alternate. Each is held every four years, but they fall two years apart. And today's athletes wear clothes!

Runners compete in the men's 5,000-m (5,468-yard) race in the 2012 Summer Olympic Games.

Grab It and Run

Cheung Chau, an island near the city of Hong Kong, has an annual Bun Scrambling or Bun Snatching contest. When the gun goes off, hundreds of men scramble up three tall towers covered in buns. The higher up the tower they are when they grab a bun, the more luck they and their family will have the next year. In times of disease and famine, this was a great prize.

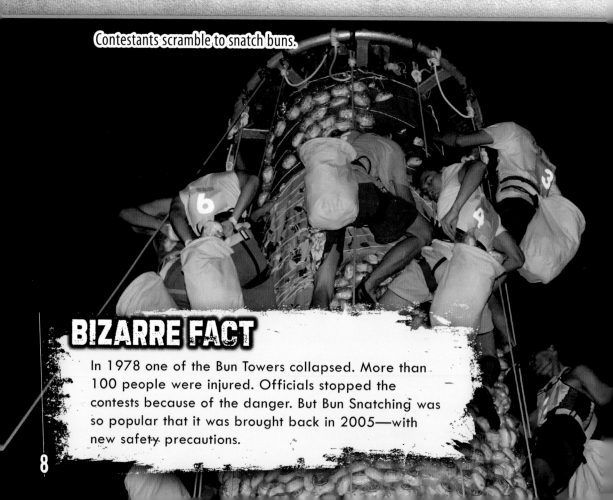

Contestants scramble to snatch buns.

BIZARRE FACT

In 1978 one of the Bun Towers collapsed. More than 100 people were injured. Officials stopped the contests because of the danger. But Bun Snatching was so popular that it was brought back in 2005—with new safety precautions.

The Wife-Carrying Championship Games have been held in Finland since 1992.

Wife Carrying

In Finland in the late 1800s, a famous outlaw trained men to rob villages. To be sure that his men were strong enough, he held wife-carrying races. This sport has since caught on. Each man carries a woman over his shoulders while racing over **obstacles** such as water and sand. Races are held today in Europe, Australia, and the Middle East as well as the United States.

> **obstacle**—something that gets in the way or prevents someone from doing something

Outhouse Races

There are many other unusual sports today. For example, outhouse races are a lot like tractor pulls. The difference? Instead of a tractor, you pull an outhouse. These races happen all across the United States. Can you imagine seeing a bunch of toilets coming down the road at you?

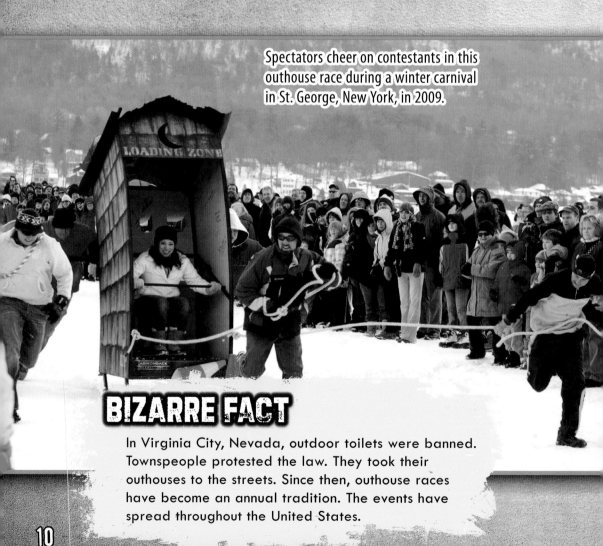

Spectators cheer on contestants in this outhouse race during a winter carnival in St. George, New York, in 2009.

BIZARRE FACT

In Virginia City, Nevada, outdoor toilets were banned. Townspeople protested the law. They took their outhouses to the streets. Since then, outhouse races have become an annual tradition. The events have spread throughout the United States.

Elephant Polo

People play elephant **polo** by riding on the backs of elephants instead of horses. Each elephant has two riders—the player and a mahout. In India, a mahout is someone paid to work with and tend elephants. The mahout's job is to steer the elephant, while the player gives directions and hits the ball.

Elephant polo became an official sport in the 1980s.

But falling off an elephant hurts more than falling off a horse. And the game can get messy when the ball gets stuck in elephant droppings!

> **polo**—a game where two teams compete to send a ball into the other team's goal; usually played on horseback but also in water

CHAPTER 2

THIS COULD LEAVE A MARK

Some people think that the threat of a little pain makes a sport more exciting.

If competition is good, a little danger can only make it better, right? No one wants to risk life and limb. But a few bumps, bruises, or even bites are usually no big deal. There are bizarre sports that will probably hurt—at least a little bit.

Shin Kicking

Shin kicking is a favorite event of the Cotswald Olimpick Games held every year in Gloucestershire, England. In shin kicking, two people grasp each other by the shoulders and then they kick one another's shins. The shins are protected only by straw padding. With each violent kick, a competitor tries to throw the other person to the ground. The first person to hit the ground loses the match.

Shin kicking is one of many sports in the Cotswald Games. These "Olimpicks" were started more than 400 years ago by Robert Dover, a local lawyer.

Buzkashi

The Persian word *buzkashi* means "goat grabbing" or "goat dragging." This game began hundreds of years ago in Central Asia. It was a way of practicing for battles and raids, when livestock was often stolen.

Horsemen compete for a goatskin at the Golden Eagle Festival in Bayan Oelgii, Mongolia, in 2012.

Buzkashi is considered the national game of Afghanistan. A dead goat is placed in the middle of a playing field. Men on horseback then try to grab the goat. They race toward a distant pole and back again to their own team. The competition can get very rough. Sometimes riders fall off their horses. The sport is still played today. Players may ride yaks instead of horses.

Pelota Purépecha

The word *pelota* means "ball" in Spanish. The
Purépecha are a people from central Mexico. Pelota
Purépecha was one of many ball games played by the
Mayans in Mexico 500 years ago. This sport was like field
hockey. But there was one important difference—the ball
was soaked in pine resin and set on fire! This game was as
dangerous as it sounds. Players were often burned. But the
night-time game was exciting for people to watch. Today
Pelota Purépecha matches are played at cultural festivals.

Today the balls used in
Pelota Purépecha are
soaked in fuel oil rather
than pine resin.

Mayans—American Indians who
lived in Mexico and
Central America
hundreds of years ago

15

Ferret Legging—Grin and Bear It

Coal miners in Yorkshire, England, in the 1970s had a little too much time on their hands. So they developed the sport of ferret legging. Male contestants would tie off the cuffs of their pants. Then they would push a sharp-toothed, and likely very annoyed, ferret down their pants. Whoever lasted the longest with a ferret down his pants won. One more thing—no underwear was allowed. In 2010 Frank Bartlett and Christine Farnsworth broke the ferret-legging record by lasting 5 hours and 30 minutes.

BIZARRE FACT

Ferrets have sharp teeth and claws. An angry one will bite and scratch, but a content ferret may just curl up for a nap.

FERRET RACING

Ferret racing began in the United States. Gas line installers used ferrets to carry lines through the pipes. They would attach equipment to the lines and thread it through the pipes. Then the crews started racing the ferrets through these pipes.

Today ferret racing is a popular sport in many countries. However, some animal rights groups protest this sport. They say it is cruel to the animals.

Cheese Rolling

Cheese rolling sounds harmless, right? In England, this bizarre sport has been going on for possibly centuries. An official rolls a large wheel of cheese down a hill, like a bowling ball.

BIZARRE FACT

Originally, the cheese used in cheese-rolling contests was English. But British cheese makers feared lawsuits from injured contestants. So they stopped supplying the cheese for these contests. Foreign cheeses, such as Gouda, have since been used.

Dutch Gouda cheese used for cheese rolling

Hundreds of competitors race after the cheese wheel and try to catch it. The cheese rolls and bounces. It sometimes reaches speeds of 70 miles (113 kilometers) per hour. The first person to reach the cheese wins.

Many people fall down the hill while chasing the cheese. These contests sometimes result in broken arms and legs. Today cheese rolling has become popular at fairs such as the Canadian Cheese Rolling Festival.

Participants in England's annual Cooper's Hill Cheese-Rolling contest race down a steep hill to catch a wheel of cheese weighing as much as 9 pounds (4 kg).

CHAPTER 3

CALL THE AMBULANCE!

Are a few bruises or a little burn not enough for you? Don't worry! Bizarre sports can give you all the danger you want. These sports go beyond the occasional "ouchie." They can easily lead to broken bones, stab wounds, or worse! Some people will try almost anything in the name of sport. To these competitors, the more dangerous a sport is, the more thrilling it is to compete in.

A rider competes in a BMX competition in Portugal in 2014.

Bull Leaping

For this bizarre sport, a person runs toward a charging bull. Then he or she quickly jumps over the animal's back. Pictures of this sport date from as early as 1400 BC in Minoan Crete. The bull usually has a full set of horns. One bad move, and the bull leaper could be stabbed by the horns or trampled by the hooves. In southern France, people play a safer version of this sport. They use young cows instead of bulls.

BIZARRE FACT

Bull leaping often appears in paintings and sculptures from the Greek Bronze Age (3300 BC to 1100 BC).

A contestant seems to fly over the bull in this bull-leaping event held in Dax, France, in 2014.

Charreada

In Mexico, a *charreada* is very similar to a rodeo. Dating from the 1500s, *charreadas* were held on ranches to display the ranch hands' skills. Today the event starts with a big parade. It has several contests, such as bull riding and team roping. In total there are nine events for men and one women's event.

A *charro* prepares to throw his lasso in a roping event in Bajio, Mexico, in 2014.

El Paso de la Muerte (The Pass of Death)

One popular event at a *charreada* is *el paso de la muerte*, or "the pass of death." In it a *charro*, or horseman, begins by riding his horse **bareback**. Then he leaps from his own horse onto the bare back of a wild horse. This horse has no saddle and no reins. The *charro* must stay on that horse until it stops bucking.

This event is very dangerous. It is easy to fall and get trampled. But some *charros* perform the sport backward to show off their skill.

BIZARRE FACT

According to Mexican law, it is illegal to win money for competing in a *charreada*. Instead *charros* can win prizes, such as saddles or horse trailers.

bareback—riding a horse or other animal without a saddle

CHAPTER 4
GAMES OF LIFE OR DEATH

Gladiator games were popular throughout the Roman Empire from about 250 BC until AD 400.

Some people like to compete so much that they will risk their lives in a sport. Some, such as Ancient Roman **gladiators**, were forced to compete. But others choose to risk life and limb. They may enjoy the **spectacle**. Or they may compete for prizes. In these bizarre sports, the winner takes all—and the loser takes the fall.

gladiator—someone trained to fight with weapons against other men or wild animals in an arena
spectacle—a public show or display on a large scale

Humans Against Beasts

Ancient Romans loved a dangerous spectacle. Gladiators were trained fighters. They often were slaves who pleased crowds by fighting in an arena. One event was a staged hunt. The emperor would bring in ferocious wild beasts to face the gladiators. Lions, tigers, crocodiles, and other beasts would fight for their lives in these events. The gladiators had weapons. The animals had claws, teeth, and instincts. After the event, the crowd would share the meat of the animal.

This modern woodcut depicts a gladiator fighting a hungry lion in Circus Maximus in Ancient Rome.

BIZARRE FACT

In one year (AD 108–109), the Roman emperor Trajan staged spectacles using 10,000 gladiators and 11,000 wild animals.

Viking Skin Pulling

For the ancient Vikings, all sports prepared them for war. Skin pulling was a form of tug-of-war between two teams. Animal skins were stitched together to make a rope. But unlike tug-of-war, this game was played over an open pit of fire! The losing team would often fall into the fire and die. The winners claimed their homes, belongings, and even families.

Modern-day "warriors" meet at Moesgaard, Denmark, every summer to recreate the festive markets and games of the ancient Vikings.

Sailors compete in a tug-of-war in 2013 in Riga, Latvia, during the Tall Ships Races annual regatta.

TUG-OF-WAR

Tug-of-war is a contest of strength between two teams. Each team pulls on a rope. The team that pulls the other team over a line or object, wins.

Tug-of-war is one of the oldest sports in history. It dates back thousands of years. It was an Olympic sport between 1900 and 1920. The Tug of War International Federation (TWIF) was founded in 1960. It now has more than 50 member countries. Its headquarters is in Wisconsin, USA.

Tug-of-war seems like a simple and safe pastime. But over the years, many contestants have suffered serious injuries. Some have lost fingers. Others have even had their arms or legs torn off!

Life and Death on the Water

In Ancient Egypt, fishermen would joust by trying to knock each other out of their boats. In the strong currents of the Nile River, this bizarre sport could turn deadly. A competitor who could not swim well might drown. He might even be eaten by crocodiles! Today safer forms of water jousting are popular in some parts of Europe.

Water jousting is one popular event during the Festival of St. Louis. It is held in the French resort town of Sète every August.

This 1894 painting shows a staged naval battle from Roman times.

Staged Naval Battles

The Ancient Romans loved a good battle. Some of the best battles took place at sea. Roman rulers sometimes staged battles as entertainment. The fighting could be in a river or an arena. It did not end until one side destroyed the other side's ships. The fighters were not trained sailors. Many were criminals and slaves. Roman citizens were excited to watch these staged battles.

Weird and dangerous sports might seem like a thing of the past. But people play bizarre sports in today's world too. Bizarre sports are here to stay!

BIZARRE FACT

The Colosseum in Rome was a marvel of architecture. It could hold more than 50,000 spectators. The Romans staged naval battles there by flooding the arena floor. The arena could hold two fleets of specially built ships. These ships had very shallow bottoms.

29

GLOSSARY

bareback (BAIR-bak)—riding a horse or other animal without a saddle

gladiator (GLAD-ee-ay-tur)—someone trained to fight with weapons against other men or wild animals in an arena

jousting (JOW-sting)—fighting between two knights on horseback with long spears called lances

Mayans (MEYE-ahnss)—American Indians who lived in Mexico and Central America hundreds of years ago

obstacle (OB-stuh-kuhl)—something that gets in the way or prevents someone from doing something

opponent (uh-POH-nuhnt)—a person who competes against another person

polo (POH-loh)—a game where two teams compete to send a ball into the other team's goal; usually played on horseback but also in water

spectacle (SPEK-tuh-kuhl)—a public show or display on a large scale

spectator (SPEK-tay-tur)—a person who attends and watches an event

stamina (STAM-uh-nuh)—the energy and strength to keep doing something for a long time

tournament (TUR-nuh-muhnt)—a series of matches between several players or teams, ending in one winner

READ MORE

Birmingham, Maria. *Weird Zone: Sports.* Toronto: Owlkids Books, 2013.

Teitelbaum, Michael. *Weird Sports.* Santa Barbara, Calif.: Beach Ball Books, 2011.

Watson, S. B. *Weird Sports of the World.* North Mankato, Minn.: The Child's World, 2014.

INTERNET SITES

FactHound offers a safe, fun way to find Internet sites related to this book. All of the sites on FactHound have been researched by our staff.

Here's all you do:

Visit *www.facthound.com*

Type in this code: 9781491442678

Check out projects, games, and lots more at
www.capstonekids.com

Index